little one's Ponchos™

Contents

Playful in
Pink
Poncho

DESIGN BY **FRANCES HUGHES**

SKILL LEVEL

EASY

FINISHED SIZES
Instructions given fit size 6–12 months *(small)*; changes for 12–18 months *(medium)* and 18–24 months *(large)* are in [ ].

MATERIALS
- Sublime Cashmere Merino Silk DK light (DK) weight yarn (127 yds/ 50g per ball):
  3 [3, 4] balls #09 blush
- Size G/6/4mm crochet hook or size needed to obtain gauge
- Tapestry needle

GAUGE
4 sts = 1 inch

PATTERN NOTE
Chain-3 at beginning of row or round counts as first double crochet unless otherwise stated.

SPECIAL STITCHES
Popcorn (pc): 4 sc in place indicated, drop lp from hook, insert hook in first st of group, pull dropped lp through, ch 1 to close.

Pigtail: Ch 10, 3 sc in each ch across, sl st in next st.

INSTRUCTIONS
PONCHO

Row 1: Beg at neck edge, ch 52 [62, 72], sc in 2nd ch from hook and in each ch across, turn. *(51 [61, 71] sc)*

Row 2: Ch 4 *(counts as first dc and ch-1)*, sk next st, dc in next st, [ch 1, sk next st, dc in next st] across, turn.

Row 3: Ch 1, sc in first st, sc in each ch and in each st across, turn.

Row 4: **Ch 3** *(see Pattern Note)*, dc in same st, [dc in each of next 9 sts, 3 dc in next st] across to last 10 sts, dc in each of next 9 sts, 2 dc in last st, turn. *(61 [71, 81] dc)*

Row 5: Ch 1, sc in each st across, turn.

Row 6: Ch 3, dc in same st, [dc in each of next 11 [14, 17] sts, 3 dc in next st] across to last 12 [10, 8] sts, dc in each of next 11 [9, 7] sts, 2 dc in last st, turn. *(71 [81, 91] dc)*

Row 7: Rep row 5.

Row 8: Ch 3, dc in same st, [dc in each of next 13 [16, 19] sts, 3 dc in next st] across to last 14 [12, 10] sts, dc in each of next 13 [11, 9] sts, 2 dc in last st, turn. *(81 [91, 101] dc)*

Row 9: Rep row 5.

Row 10: Ch 3, dc in same st, [dc in each of next 15 [18, 21] sts, 3 dc in next st] across to last 16 [14, 12] sts, dc in each of next 15 [13, 11] sts, 2 dc in last st, turn. *(91 [101, 111] dc)*

Row 11: Rep row 5.

Row 12: Ch 3, dc in same st, [dc in each of next 17 [20, 23] sts, 3 dc in next st] across to last 18 [16, 14] sts, dc in each of next 17 [15, 13] sts, 2 dc in last st, turn. *(101 [111, 121] dc)*

Row 13: Rep row 5.

Row 14: Ch 3, dc in same st, [dc in each of next 19 [22, 25] sts, 3 dc in next st] across to last 20 [18, 16] sts, dc in each of next 19 [17, 15] sts, 2 dc in last st, turn. *(111 [121, 131] dc)*

Row 15: Rep row 5.

Row 16: Ch 3, dc in same st, [dc in each of next 21 [24, 27] sts, 3 dc in next st] across to last 22 [20, 18] sts, dc in each of next 21 [19, 17] sts, 2 dc in last st, turn. *(121 [131, 141] dc)*

Row 17: Rep row 5.

Row 18: Ch 3, dc in same st, *dc in each st across to center st of next 3-dc group**, 3 dc in next st, rep from * across, ending last rep at **, 2 dc in last st, turn. *(131 [141, 151] dc)*

Row 19: Rep row 5.

Next rows: Rep rows 18 and 19 alternately until piece measures 7 [9, 10] inches from beg, ending with row 19. At end of last row, **do not fasten off**.

EDGING
Ch 1, sc in first st, [**pc** *(see Special Stitches)* in next st, sl st in each of next 3 sts, **pigtail** *(see Special Stitches)* in next st, sl st in each of next 2 sts] across, ending last rep as needed at end of row. Fasten off.

NECK TIE
Ch 121 or desired length, 3 sc in 2nd ch from hook and in each of next 9 chs, sc in each ch across to last 10 chs, 3 sc in each of last 10 chs. Fasten off.

Weave Neck Tie through ch sps on row 2.

Sew ends of rows tog from bottom edge up the center front, leaving 3 inches or more opening at neck edge.

Tie ends of Neck Tie into bow. ∎

Spring Flowers
Poncho

DESIGN BY **SUE CHILDRESS**

SKILL LEVEL

■■□□
EASY

FINISHED SIZES

Instructions given fit size 6–12 months *(small)*; changes for 12–18 months *(medium)* and 18–24 months *(large)* are in [ ].

MATERIALS

- Schachenmayr Nomotta Catania fine (sport) weight yarn (137 yds/ 50g per skein):
  2 [3, 4] skeins #204 bright yellow
  1 skein each #143 salmon, #114 hot pink, #113 purple, #211 burgundy and #163 light green
- Size G/6/4mm crochet hook or size needed to obtain gauge
- Tapestry needle

GAUGE

4 sts = 1 inch

PATTERN NOTES

Join with slip stitch as indicated unless otherwise stated.

Chain-3 at beginning of row or round counts as first double crochet unless otherwise stated.

Chain-2 at beginning of row or round counts as first half double crochet unless otherwise stated.

SPECIAL STITCHES

Beginning shell (beg shell): Ch 3 *(see Pattern Notes)*, (dc, ch 2, 2 dc) in place indicated.

Shell: (2 dc, ch 2, 2 dc) in place indicated.

INSTRUCTIONS
PONCHO

Rnd 1: With bright yellow, ch 80 [88, 96], sl st in first ch to form ring, **ch 2** *(see Pattern Notes)*, hdc in each ch around, **join** *(see Pattern Notes)* in 2nd ch of beg ch-2. *(80 [88, 96] hdc)*

Rnd 2: Ch 2, hdc in same st, hdc in next st, [2 hdc in next st, hdc in next st] around, join in 2nd ch of beg ch-2. *(120 [132,144] hdc)*

Rnd 3: **Beg shell** *(see Special Stitches)* in first st, dc in each of next 29 [32, 35] sts, [**shell** *(see Special Stitches)* in next st, dc in each of next 29 [32, 35] sts] around, join in 3rd ch of beg ch-3. *(4 shells, 116 [128, 140] dc)*

Rnds 4–7: Sl st in next st, sl st in next ch-2 sp, beg shell in same ch sp, *dc in each st across to next ch-2 sp including sts of shells **, shell in next ch-2 sp, rep from * around, ending last rep at **, join in 3rd ch of beg ch-3. *(4 shells, 180 [192, 204] dc at end of last rnd)*

Rnds 8–11: Sl st in next st, sl st in next ch-2 sp, beg shell in same ch sp, *skipping sts of shells, dc in each st across to next shell**, shell in ch sp of next shell, rep from * around, ending last rep at **, join in 3rd ch of beg ch-3.

Rnd 12: Sl st in next st, sl st in next ch-2 sp, (beg shell, ch 2, 2 dc) in same ch sp, *skipping sts of shells, dc in each st across to next shell**, (shell, ch 2, 2 dc) in ch sp of next shell, rep from * around, ending last rep at **, join in 3rd ch of beg ch-3.

Rnd 13: Sl st in next st, sl st in next ch-2 sp, beg shell in same ch sp, shell in next ch-2 sp, *skipping sts of shells, dc in each st across to next shell**, shell in ch sp of next shell, shell in next ch-2 sp, rep from * around, ending last rep at **, join in 3rd ch of beg ch-3.

Rnd 14: Ch 1, sc in each st around with 2 sc in each ch-2 sp, join in beg sc. Fasten off.

NECK EDGING

Rnd 1: Working in starting ch on opposite side of rnd 1, join bright yellow with sc in any ch, sc in each of next 2 chs, sk next ch, [sc in each of next 3 chs, sk next ch] around, join in beg sc. *(60 [66, 72] sc)*

Rnd 2: Ch 1, sc in each of first 5 sts, sk next st, [sc in each of next 5 sts, sk next st] around, join in beg sc. *(50 [55, 60] sc)*

Rnd 3: Ch 1, sc in each st around, join in beg sc. Fasten off.

FLOWER
MAKE 4 EACH OF SALMON, HOT PINK, PURPLE AND BURGUNDY.

Rnd 1: Ch 3, working over end of yarn, 11 hdc in 3rd ch from hook *(first 2 chs count as first hdc)*, join in 2nd ch of beg ch-2, pull yarn end to close ring. *(12 hdc)*

Rnd 2: [Ch 3, **fpsc** *(see Stitch Guide)* around next st] around, ch 3, join in first ch of beg ch-3. Fasten off.

LEAF
MAKE 5.

With light green, ch 6, hdc in 3rd ch from hook, hdc in next ch, sc in each of last 2 chs. Fasten off.

FINISHING

Poncho will need blocking with steam iron or wet block.

Arrange and sew Flowers and Leaves around neck as shown in photo. ∎

Shells & Picots Poncho

DESIGN BY FRANCES HUGHES

SKILL LEVEL

EASY

FINISHED SIZES

Instructions given fit size 6–12 months (*small*); changes for 12–18 months (*medium*) and 18–24 months (*large*) are in [ ].

MATERIALS

- Berroco Pure Merino medium (worsted) weight yarn (92 yds/ 50g per ball):
    3 [3, 4] balls #8555 cardinal
- Size G/6/4mm crochet hook or size needed to obtain gauge
- ¼-inch red ribbon: 1½ yds

GAUGE

4 sts = 1 inch

PATTERN NOTES

Join with slip stitch as indicated unless otherwise stated.

Chain-3 at beginning of row or round counts as first double crochet unless otherwise stated.

SPECIAL STITCHES

Cluster (cl): Holding back last lp of each st on hook, 3 dc in place indicated, yo, pull through all lps on hook.

Beginning small shell (beg sm shell): Ch 3, (dc, ch 2, 2 dc) in same place.

Small Shell (sm shell): (2 dc, ch 2, 2 dc) in place indicated.

V-stitch (V-st): (Dc, ch 1, dc) in place indicated.

Beginning large shell (beg lg shell): Ch 3, (2 dc, ch 2, 3 dc) in same place.

Large shell (lg shell): (3 dc, ch 2, 3 dc) in place indicated.

Picot: Ch 4, sl st in 4th ch from hook.

INSTRUCTIONS
PONCHO

Rnd 1: Beg at neck, ch 42 [51, 60], sl st in first ch to form ring, **ch 3** *(see Pattern Notes)*, dc in each ch around, **join** *(see Pattern Notes)* in 3rd ch of beg ch-3.

Rnd 2: Beg sm shell *(see Special Stitches)* in first st, *ch 1, sk next 2 sts**, **sm shell** *(see Special Stitches)* in next st, rep from * around, ending last rep at **, join in 3rd ch of beg ch-3. *(14 [17, 20] shells)*

Rnd 3: Sl st in next st and in next ch sp, beg sm shell in same ch sp, **V-st** *(see Special Stitches)* in next ch-1 sp, [shell in ch sp of next shell, V-st in next ch-1 sp] around, join in 3rd ch of beg ch-3.

Rnds 4–7: Sl st in next st and in next ch sp, beg sm shell in same ch sp, V-st in ch sp of next V-st, [sm shell in ch sp of next shell, V-st in ch sp of next V-st] around, join in 3rd ch of beg ch-3.

Rnd 8: Sl st in next st and in next ch sp, **beg lg shell** *(see Special Stitches)* in same ch sp, V-st in ch sp of next V-st, [**lg shell** *(see Special Stitches)* in ch sp of next sm shell, V-st in ch sp of next V-st] around, join in 3rd ch of beg ch-3.

Rnds 9 & 10: Sl st in next 2 sts and in next ch sp, beg lg shell in same ch sp, V-st in ch sp of next V-st, [lg shell in ch sp of next lg shell, V-st in ch sp of next V-st] around, join in 3rd ch of beg ch-3.

Rnd 11: Ch 3, dc in each of next 2 sts, (2 tr, **picot**–*see Special Stitches*, 2 tr) in ch sp of this lg shell, dc in each of next 3 dc of same shell, **cl** *(see Special Stitches)* in ch sp of next V-st, [(dc in each of next 3 dc of next lg shell, (2 tr, picot, 2 tr) in ch sp of same lg shell, dc in each of next 3 sts of same shell, cl in ch sp of next V-st] around, join in 3rd ch of beg ch-3. Fasten off.

FINISHING
Weave ribbon through sts on rnd 1.

Tie ends of ribbon tog in bow.

Tie knot in each end of ribbon. ■

Fancy Collar Poncho

DESIGN BY **SUE CHILDRESS**

SKILL LEVEL

EASY

FINISHED SIZES

Instructions given fit size 6–12 months *(small)*; changes for 12–18 months *(medium)* and 18–24 months *(large)* are in [ ].

MATERIALS

- Ella Rae Extrafine Heathers medium (worsted) weight yarn (85 yds/50g per ball):
  3 [4, 5] balls #04 lilac blush
- Trendsetter Ballet bulky (chunky) weight (65 yds/50g per skein):
  1 skein #400 white
- Size G/6/4mm crochet hook or size needed to obtain gauge

GAUGE

4 sts = 1 inch

PATTERN NOTES

Chain-3 at beginning of row or round counts as first double crochet unless otherwise stated.

Join with slip stitch as indicated unless otherwise stated.

SPECIAL STITCH

Shell: (2 dc, ch 2, 2 dc) in place indicated.

INSTRUCTIONS

PONCHO

Rnd 1: Beg at neck edge, with lilac blush, ch 75 [85, 95], being careful not to twist ch, sl st in first ch to form ring, **ch 3** *(see Pattern Notes)*, dc in each of next 3 chs, 2 dc in next ch, [dc in each of next 4 chs, 2 dc in next ch] 14 times, dc in each of last 0 [10, 20] sts, **join** *(see Pattern Notes)* in 3rd ch of beg ch-3. *(90 [100, 110] dc)*

Rnd 2: Ch 3, dc in each of next 3 sts, **shell** *(see Special Stitch)* in next st, [dc in each of next 4 sts, shell in next st] around, join in 3rd ch of beg ch-3. *(18 [20, 22] shells)*

Rnd 3: Ch 3, [dc in each st across to next shell, **do not work** in sts of shells, shell in ch sp of next shell, **do not work** in sts of shell] around, join in beg ch-3.

Rnds 4–12 [4–14, 4–16]: Rep rnd 3.

Last rnd: *[Ch 3, sc in next st] across to next shell, **do not work** in sts of shell, 5 dc in ch sp of next shell, **do not work** in sts of shell, rep from * around, join in first ch of beg ch-3. Fasten off.

NECK EDGING

Working in starting ch on opposite side of rnd 1, holding 2 strands of white tog, join with sc in any ch, sc in each of next 3 chs, sk next ch, [sc in each of next 4 chs, sk next ch] around, join in beg sc. Fasten off. ■

Cross-Stitch Poncho

DESIGN BY **FRANCES HUGHES**

SKILL LEVEL

EASY

FINISHED SIZES

Instructions given fit size 6–12 months *(small)*; changes for 12–18 months *(medium)* and 18–24 months *(large)* are in [ ].

MATERIALS

- Sirdar Snuggly Dk light (DK) weight yarn (191 yds/50g per ball): 3 [3, 4] balls #260 summer lime
- Size G/6/4mm crochet hook or size needed to obtain gauge
- Tapestry needle

3 LIGHT

GAUGE

4 sts = 1 inch; 6 pattern rows = 2 inches

PATTERN NOTES

Chain-3 at beginning of row or round counts as first double crochet unless otherwise stated.

Join with slip stitch as indicated unless otherwise stated.

SPECIAL STITCH

Cross-stitch (cross-st): Sk next st, dc in next st, working over last st, dc in st just sk.

INSTRUCTIONS
PONCHO
RECTANGULAR PIECE
MAKE 2.

Row 1: Ch 71 [89, 107], sc in 2nd ch from hook and in each ch across, turn. *(70 [88, 106] dc)*

Row 2: Ch 3 *(see Pattern Notes)*, [**cross-st** *(see Special Stitch)*, dc in next st] across, turn. *(23 [29, 35] cross sts, 24 [30, 36] dc)*

Row 3: Ch 1, sc in each st across, turn.

Next rows: [Rep rows 2 and 3 alternately] 11 [13, 15] times. At end of last row, fasten off.

ASSEMBLY

Sew starting ch of First Rectangular Piece to ends of rows on 2nd Rectangular Piece *(see Assembly Diagram)*.

Matching colored Xs on Assembly Diagram, sew 2nd Rectangular Piece to First Rectangular Piece.

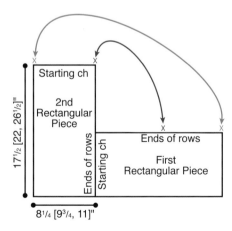

Cross-Stitch Poncho
Assembly Diagram

BOTTOM EDGING

Rnd 1: Working in sts and ends of rows, join with sc in any st, evenly sp sc around with 3 sc in each corner, **join** (see Pattern Notes) in beg sc.

Rnd 2: Ch 1, sc in first st, ch 5, sk next st, [sc in next st, ch 5, sk next st] around, join in beg sc.

Rnd 3: [Ch 5, working in front of next ch sp, sc in next sk st, ch 5, working in back of next ch sp, sc in next sk st] around, join in joining sl st of last rnd. Fasten off.

NECK EDGING

Working in ends of rows around neck opening, join with sc in any row, working from left to right, evenly sp **reverse sc** (see Stitch Guide) around, join in beg sc. Fasten off.

BOW

Ch 55, 8 dc in 3rd ch from hook, loosely sl st in each ch across to last ch, 8 dc in last ch. Fasten off.

Tie in Bow and sew to neck edge at center front of Poncho. ∎

Lil Collar
Poncho

DESIGN BY **SUE CHILDRESS**

SKILL LEVEL

EASY

FINISHED SIZES

Instructions given fit size 6–12 months *(small)*; changes for 12–18 months *(medium)* and 18–24 months *(large)* are in [ ].

MATERIALS

- Berroco Comfort medium (worsted) weight yarn (210 yds/100g per ball): 2 [2, 3] balls #9736 primary blue
- Size G/6/4mm crochet hook or size needed to obtain gauge
- Tapestry needle
- Decorative button

GAUGE

4 sts = 1 inch

PATTERN NOTES

Chain-3 at beginning of row or round counts as first double crochet unless otherwise stated.

Join with slip stitch as indicated unless otherwise stated.

INSTRUCTIONS
PONCHO

Row 1: Beg at neck, ch 41 [51, 61], hdc in 3rd ch from hook *(first 2 chs count as first hdc)* and in each ch across, turn. *(40 [50, 60] hdc)*

Row 2: **Ch 3** *(see Pattern Notes)*, dc in each of next 2 sts, ch 3, sk next st, sc in each of next 2 sts, ch 3, sk next st, [dc in each of next 6 sts, ch 3, sk next st, sc in each of next 2 sts, sk next st, ch 3] across to last 3 sts, dc in each of last 3 sts, turn.

Row 3: Ch 3, dc in next st, 2 dc in next st, ch 3, sc in next ch-3 sp, sc in each of next 2 sts, sc in next ch-3 sp, ch 3, [2 dc in next st, dc in each of next 4 sts, 2 dc in next st, ch 3, sc in next ch-3 sp, sc in each of next 2 sts, sc in next ch-3 sp, ch 3] across to last 3 sts, 2 dc in next st, dc in each of last 2 sts, turn.

Row 4: Ch 3, dc in each of next 2 sts, 2 dc in next st, ch 3, sc in next st, ch 3, sk next 2 sts, sc in next st, ch 3, [2 dc in next st, dc in each of next 6 sts, 2 dc in next st, ch 3, sc in next st, ch 3, sk next 2 sts, sc in next st, ch 3] across to last 4 sts, 2 dc in next st, dc in each of last 3 sts, turn.

Row 5: Ch 3, dc in each of next 3 sts, 2 dc in next st, ch 3, sc in next ch-3 sp, ch 3, 2 sc in next ch-3 sp, ch 3, sc in next ch-3 sp, ch 3, [2 dc in next st, dc in each of next 8 sts, 2 dc in next st, ch 3, sc in next ch-3 sp, ch 3, 2 sc in next ch-3 sp, ch 3, sc in next ch-3 sp] across to last 5 sts, 2 dc in next st, dc in each of last 4 sts, turn.

Row 6: Ch 3, dc in each of next 4 sts, 2 dc in next st, *[ch 3, sc in next ch-3 sp] twice, sc in each of next 2 sts, [sc in next ch-3 sp, ch 3] twice**, 2 dc in next st, dc in each of next 10 sts, 2 dc in next st, rep from * across, ending last rep at **, 2 dc in next st, dc in each of last 5 sts, turn.

Row 7: Ch 3, dc in each of next 5 sts, 2 dc in next st, ch 3, sc in next ch-3 sp, ch 3, sk next ch-3 sp, dc in each of next 4 sts, ch 3, sk next ch-3 sp, sc in next ch-3 sp, ch 3, [2 dc in next st, dc in each of next 12 sts, 2 dc in next st, ch 3, sc in next ch-3 sp, ch 3, sk next ch-3 sp, dc in each of next 4 sts, ch 3, sk next ch-3 sp, sc in next ch-3 sp, ch 3] across to last 7 sts, 2 dc in next st, dc in each of last 6 sts, turn.

Row 8: Ch 3, dc in same st, dc in each of next 6 sts, 2 dc in next st, ch 3, sc in next ch-3 sp, ch 3, dc in next ch-3 sp, dc in each of next 4 sts, dc in next ch-3 sp, ch 3, sc in next ch-3 sp, ch 3, [dc in each of next 6 sts, ch 3, sk next st, sc in each of next 2 sts, ch 3, sk next st, dc in each of next 6 sts, ch 3, sc in next ch-3 sp, ch 3, dc in next ch-3 sp, dc in each of next 4 sts, dc in next ch-3 sp, ch 3, sc in next ch-3 sp, ch 3] across to last 8 sts, 2 dc in next st, dc in each of next 6 sts, 2 dc in next st, turn.

Row 9: Ch 3, dc in each of next 9 sts, [ch 3, sc in next ch-3 sp] twice, ch 3, dc in each of next 6 sts, [ch 3, sc in next ch-3 sp] twice, ch 3, *dc in each of next 6 sts, ch 3, sc in next ch-3 sp, ch 3, dc in each of next 2 sts, ch 3, sc in next ch sp, ch 3, dc in each of next 6 sts, [ch 3, sc in next ch-3 sp] twice, ch 3, dc in each of next 6 sts, [ch 3, sc in next ch-3 sp] twice, ch 3, rep from * across, ending with dc in each of last 10 sts, turn.

Row 10: Ch 3, dc in each of next 9 sts, [ch 3, sc in next ch-3 sp] 3 times, ch 3, dc in each of next 6 sts, [ch 3, sc in next ch-3 sp] 3 times, ch 3, *dc in each of next 6 sts, [ch 3, sc in next ch-3 sp] twice, ch 3, dc in each of next 2 sts, [ch 3, sc in next ch-3 sp] twice, ch 3, dc in each of next 6 sts, [ch 3, sc in next ch-3 sp] 3 times, ch 3, dc in each of next 6 sts, [ch 3, sc in next ch-3 sp] 3 times, ch 3, rep from * across, ending with dc in each of last 10 sts, turn.

Row 11: Ch 3, dc in each of next 9 sts, work the following steps to complete this rnd:

A. Ch 3, sk next ch-3 sp, [ch 3, sc in next ch-3 sp] twice;

B. Ch 3, sk next ch-3 sp, dc in each of next 6 sts;

C. Rep steps A, B and A;

D. Sk next 2 sts, [sc in next ch-3 sp, ch 3] twice;

E. Rep step B;

F. Rep steps A–E across, ending last rep with step C;

G. Dc in each of last 10 sts, turn.

Row 12: Ch 3, dc in each of next 9 sts, ◊*[ch 3, sc in next ch-3 sp] 3 times, ch 3, dc in each of next 6 sts*, rep between * once, [ch 3, sc in next ch-3 sp] 5 times, ch 3, dc in each of next 6 sts, rep from ◊ across, [ch 3, sc in next ch-3 sp] 3 times, dc in each of last 10 sts, turn.

Row 13: Ch 3, dc in each of next 9 sts, ◊*sk next ch-3 sp, [ch 3, sc in next ch-3 sp] twice, ch 3, sk next ch-3 sp, dc in each of next 6 sts, ch 3**, rep from * once, sk next ch-3 sp, [sc in next ch-3 sp, ch 3] 4 times, sk next ch-3 sp, dc in each of next 6 sts, rep from ◊ across, ending last rep at **, sk next ch sp, [sc in next ch sp, ch 3] twice, sk next ch sp, dc in each of last 10 sts, turn.

Row 14: Rep row 12.

Next rows: [Rep rows 13 and 14 alternately] 1 [2, 3] time(s).

Next row: Ch 4, [sk next st, sc in next st, ch 4] 4 times, [sc in next ch-3 sp, ch 4] 4 times, [sk next st, sc in next st, ch 4] 3 times, [sc in next ch-3 sp, ch 4] 3 times, [sk next st, sc in next st, ch 4] 3 times, [sc in next ch-3 sp, ch 4] 6 times, [sk next st, sc in next st, ch 4] 3 times, [sc in next ch-3 sp, ch 4] 4 times, continue in this pattern across, **do not turn**.

Last row: Holding ends of rows tog, working through both thicknesses and in ends of rows, evenly sp sl sts across, leaving first 5 rows at neck edge open. Fasten off.

EDGING

Working in starting ch on opposite side of row 1 and in ends of first 5 rows on front, join with sc in first ch on right edge, sc in each ch across, evenly sp sc in ends of first 5 rows, sc in end of last row on Poncho, evenly sp sc in ends of first 5 rows, ch 5 *(button loop)*, **join** *(see Pattern Notes)* in beg sc.

COLLAR

Row 1: Working in **back lps** *(see Stitch Guide)*, ch 3, dc in each st across to opposite side of neck edge, leaving rem sts on front unworked, turn.

Row 2: Working in both lps, ch 3, dc in each st across, turn.

Row 3: Ch 1, sc in each st across, **do not turn**.

Row 4: Working in ends of rows, sl st in end of each row across Collar, **turn**, evenly sp [ch 4, sc in next st] 3 times up to corner, [ch 4, sk next st, sc in next st] across Collar, evenly sp [ch 4, sc in end of next row] 3 times down ends of rows on Collar, sl st in next st. Fasten off.

Sew button opposite button loop on Edging. ∎

STITCH GUIDE

STITCH ABBREVIATIONS

beg	begin/begins/beginning
bpdc	back post double crochet
bpsc	back post single crochet
bptr	back post treble crochet
CC	contrasting color
ch(s)	chain(s)
ch-	refers to chain or space previously made (i.e., ch-1 space)
ch sp(s)	chain space(s)
cl(s)	cluster(s)
cm	centimeter(s)
dc	double crochet (singular/plural)
dc dec	double crochet 2 or more stitches together, as indicated
dec	decrease/decreases/decreasing
dtr	double treble crochet
ext	extended
fpdc	front post double crochet
fpsc	front post single crochet
fptr	front post treble crochet
g	gram(s)
hdc	half double crochet
hdc dec	half double crochet 2 or more stitches together, as indicated
inc	increase/increases/increasing
lp(s)	loop(s)
MC	main color
mm	millimeter(s)
oz	ounce(s)
pc	popcorn(s)
rem	remain/remains/remaining
rep(s)	repeat(s)
rnd(s)	round(s)
RS	right side
sc	single crochet (singular/plural)
sc dec	single crochet 2 or more stitches together, as indicated
sk	skip/skipped/skipping
sl st(s)	slip stitch(es)
sp(s)	space(s)/spaced
st(s)	stitch(es)
tog	together
tr	treble crochet
trtr	triple treble
WS	wrong side
yd(s)	yard(s)
yo	yarn over

YARN CONVERSION

OUNCES TO GRAMS		GRAMS TO OUNCES	
1	28.4	25	⅞
2	56.7	40	1⅔
3	85.0	50	1¾
4	113.4	100	3½

UNITED STATES		UNITED KINGDOM
sl st (slip stitch)	=	sc (single crochet)
sc (single crochet)	=	dc (double crochet)
hdc (half double crochet)	=	htr (half treble crochet)
dc (double crochet)	=	tr (treble crochet)
tr (treble crochet)	=	dtr (double treble crochet)
dtr (double treble crochet)	=	ttr (triple treble crochet)
skip	=	miss

Single crochet decrease (sc dec): (Insert hook, yo, draw lp through) in each of the sts indicated, yo, draw through all lps on hook.

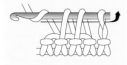

Example of 2-sc dec

Half double crochet decrease (hdc dec): (Yo, insert hook, yo, draw lp through) in each of the sts indicated, yo, draw through all lps on hook.

Example of 2-hdc dec

Reverse Single Crochet (reverse sc): Ch 1. Skip first st. [Working from left to right, insert hook in next st from front to back, draw up lp on hook, yo, and draw through both lps on hook.]

Chain (ch): Yo, pull through lp on hook.

Single crochet (sc): Insert hook in st, yo, pull through st, yo, pull through both lps on hook.

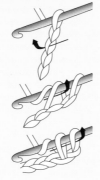

Double crochet (dc): Yo, insert hook in st, yo, pull through st, [yo, pull through 2 lps] twice.

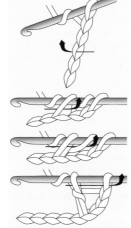

Double crochet decrease (dc dec): Yo, insert hook, yo, draw loop through, draw through 2 lps on hook) in each of the sts indicated, yo, draw through all lps on hook.

Example of 2-dc dec

Front loop (front lp) Back loop (back lp)

Front Loop   Back Loop

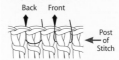

Front post stitch (fp): Back post stitch (bp): When working post st, insert hook from right to left around post st on previous row.

Back   Front

Post of Stitch

Half double crochet (hdc): Yo, insert hook in st, yo, pull through st, yo, pull through all 3 lps on hook.

Double treble crochet (dtr): Yo 3 times, insert hook in st, yo, pull through st, [yo, pull through 2 lps] 4 times.

Treble crochet decrease (tr dec): Holding back last lp of each st, tr in each of the sts indicated, yo, pull through all lps on hook.

Example of 2-tr dec

Slip stitch (sl st): Insert hook in st, pull through both lps on hook.

Chain Color Change (ch color change) Yo with new color, draw through last lp on hook.

Double Crochet Color Change (dc color change) Drop first color, yo with new color, draw through last 2 lps of st.

Treble crochet (tr): Yo twice, insert hook in st, yo, pull through st, [yo, pull through 2 lps] 3 times.

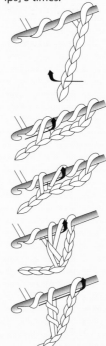

Metric
Conversion
Charts

METRIC CONVERSIONS

yards	x	.9144	=	metres (m)
yards	x	91.44	=	centimetres (cm)
inches	x	2.54	=	centimetres (cm)
inches	x	25.40	=	millimetres (mm)
inches	x	.0254	=	metres (m)

centimetres	x	.3937	=	inches
metres	x	1.0936	=	yards

INCHES INTO MILLIMETRES & CENTIMETRES (Rounded off slightly)

inches	mm	cm	inches	cm	inches	cm	inches	cm
1/8	3	0.3	5	12.5	21	53.5	38	96.5
1/4	6	0.6	5 1/2	14	22	56	39	99
3/8	10	1	6	15	23	58.5	40	101.5
1/2	13	1.3	7	18	24	61	41	104
5/8	15	1.5	8	20.5	25	63.5	42	106.5
3/4	20	2	9	23	26	66	43	109
7/8	22	2.2	10	25.5	27	68.5	44	112
1	25	2.5	11	28	28	71	45	114.5
1 1/4	32	3.2	12	30.5	29	73.5	46	117
1 1/2	38	3.8	13	33	30	76	47	119.5
1 3/4	45	4.5	14	35.5	31	79	48	122
2	50	5	15	38	32	81.5	49	124.5
2 1/2	65	6.5	16	40.5	33	84	50	127
3	75	7.5	17	43	34	86.5		
3 1/2	90	9	18	46	35	89		
4	100	10	19	48.5	36	91.5		
4 1/2	115	11.5	20	51	37	94		

KNITTING NEEDLES CONVERSION CHART

Canada/U.S.	0	1	2	3	4	5	6	7	8	9	10	10½	11	13	15
Metric (mm)	2	2¼	2¾	3¼	3½	3¾	4	4½	5	5½	6	6½	8	9	10

CROCHET HOOKS CONVERSION CHART

Canada/U.S.	1/B	2/C	3/D	4/E	5/F	6/G	8/H	9/I	10/J	10½/K	N
Metric (mm)	2.25	2.75	3.25	3.5	3.75	4.25	5	5.5	6	6.5	9.0

Annie's Attic®

Little One's Ponchos is published by DRG, 306 East Parr Road, Berne, IN 46711.
Printed in USA. Copyright © 2010 DRG. All rights reserved. This publication may not be
reproduced in part or in whole without written permission from the publisher.

RETAIL STORES: If you would like to carry this pattern book or any other
DRG publications, visit DRGwholesale.com

Every effort has been made to ensure that the instructions in this publication are complete and accurate.
We cannot, however, take responsibility for human error, typographical mistakes or variations
in individual work. Please visit AnniesCustomerCare.com to check for pattern updates..

ISBN: 978-1-59635-326-8

1 2 3 4 5 6 7 8 9